Indian Air Fryer Cookbook for Beginners

1000-Day Yummy Air Fryer Recipes to Fry, Bake, Grill, and Roast

from Across the Kitchens of India

Teera Lodha

Table of contents

Introduction

Cooking with air frier is safe and easy, preserving the real flavors of the ingredients and giving best of the air frying technique without the problems linked with over usage of frying oils. By making these 5-star Indian recipes at home with air fryer, you can cut down on your calories, control your cravings to eat out and start enjoying a guilt free, luscious meal with your family and friends.

Home baked in air fryer and cooked with healthy ingredients; Indian recipes presented in this cookbook are gourmet treat for any food lover. Indian recipes in this book can be made with easily available ingredients in every Kitchen and are presented in visually appealing format for home chefs. Get the best possible results from your air fryer and discover the best ways to use it!

Are you looking for an Asian cookbook all about air fryer cooking? Then look no further, as this cookbook brings you all the mouthwatering Asian recipes that you can cook in your air fryer with complete ease and convenience. Try these healthy and delicious Indian recipes today.

Chapter 1: Air Fryer Basics

What is an Air Fryer?

An air fryer is one of the magical cooking appliances which help to cook various delicious and tasty dishes at home. The air fryer works like a convection oven. It cooks food by circulating very hot air into an air fryer chamber. You can fry French fries with very less oil required. It saves more than 80percent of oil while frying or cooking food. Most of the people are disappointed due to the lack of crispiness in their food. The air fryer makes your food crispy and tasty.

Air fryer circulates hot air into food basket with the help of a fan. These fans are located on the top of the food basket. Using this fan air fryer circulates quick and even air around the food basket. Due to this, your food is cook evenly on all sides. It is one of the best choices for those people who love fried food most but also hate about the extra calories.

The Benefits of Air Fryer

The air fryer comes with various benefits some of them are described as follows:

1. **Requires less oil and fats**

    Compare to other traditional fryer Air fryer requires very less oil to fry. It saves more than 80 percent of oil during cooking. Just a tablespoon of oil fries your French fries make it tender from inside and crispy from outside.

2. **Saves nutritional values**

    Traditional deep-frying method destroys essential vitamin and minerals from your food. Air fryer fries your food by blowing the very hot air into a food basket. Air frying your food helps to maintain essential vitamins and nutrients into your food.

3. **Versatile cooking options**

Air fryer is not only used for frying purpose but also cooks, roasts, grill and bake delicious food for you. It works like a multi-cooker do all the operations into a single pot.

4. Reduce the risk of heart-related disease

Eating deep-fried food is not a healthy choice for your body. Air fryer requires very less oil to fry your food. It also maintains essential vitamins and nutrients into your food. This will help to reduce heart-related disease.

5. Automatic cooking programs

Most of the air fryer comes with pre-programmed auto cook buttons. These auto cooking functions are nothing but commonly used programs like French fries, chicken fries, chips, etc. You just need to press auto cook function button your air fryer automatically adjusts the time and temperature of your air fryer.

Chapter 2: Snack & Appetizers Recipes

Pepperoni Chips

Preparation Time: 2 minutes
Cooking Time: 8 minutes
Serve: 6

Ingredients:

- 6 oz pepperoni slices

Directions:

1. Place one batch of pepperoni slices in the air fryer basket.
2. Cook for 8 minutes at 360 F.
3. Cook remaining pepperoni slices using same steps.
4. Serve and enjoy.

Nutritional Value (Amount per Serving):

- Calories 51
- Fat 1 g
- Carbohydrates 2 g
- Sugar 1.3 g
- Protein 0 g
- Cholesterol 0 mg

Buffalo Cauliflower Wings

Preparation Time: 10 minutes
Cooking Time: 14 minutes
Serve:4

Ingredients:

- 1 cauliflower head, cut into florets
- 1 tbsp butter, melted
- 1/2 cup buffalo sauce
- Pepper
- Salt

Directions:

1. Spray air fryer basket with cooking spray.
2. In a bowl, mix together buffalo sauce, butter, pepper, and salt.
3. Add cauliflower florets into the air fryer basket and cook at 400 F for 7 minutes.
4. Transfer cauliflower florets into the buffalo sauce mixture and toss well.
5. Again, add cauliflower florets into the air fryer basket and cook for 7 minutes more at 400 F.
6. Serve and enjoy.

Nutritional Value (Amount per Serving):

- Calories 44
- Fat 3 g
- Carbohydrates 3.8 g
- Sugar 1.6 g
- Protein 1.3 g
- Cholesterol 8 mg

Air Fry Bacon

Preparation Time: 5 minutes
Cooking Time: 10 minutes
Serve:11

Ingredients:

- 11 bacon slices

Directions:

1. Place half bacon slices in air fryer basket.
2. Cook at 400 F for 10 minutes.
3. Cook remaining half bacon slices using same steps.
4. Serve and enjoy.

Nutritional Value (Amount per Serving):

- Calories 103
- Fat 7.9 g
- Carbohydrates 0.3 g
- Sugar 0 g
- Protein 7 g
- Cholesterol 21 mg

Sesame Okra

Preparation Time: 10 minutes
Cooking Time: 4 minutes
Serve: 4

Ingredients:

- 11 oz okra, wash and chop
- 1 egg, lightly beaten
- 1 tsp sesame seeds
- 1 tbsp sesame oil
- 1/4 tsp pepper
- 1/2 tsp salt

Directions:

1. In a bowl, whisk together egg, pepper, and salt.
2. Add okra into the whisked egg. Sprinkle with sesame seeds.
3. Preheat the air fryer to 400 F.
4. Stir okra well. Spray air fryer basket with cooking spray.
5. Place okra pieces into the air fryer basket and cook for 4 minutes.
6. Serve and enjoy.

Nutritional Value (Amount per Serving):

- Calories 82
- Fat 5 g
- Carbohydrates 6.2 g
- Sugar 1.2 g
- Protein 3 g
- Cholesterol 41 mg

Onion Dip

Preparation Time: 10 minutes

Cooking Time: 25 minutes

Serve: 8

Ingredients:

- 2 lbs onion, chopped
- 1/2 tsp baking soda
- 6 tbsp butter, softened
- Pepper
- Salt

Directions:

1. Melt butter in a pan over medium heat.
2. Add onion and baking soda and sauté for 5 minutes.
3. Transfer onion mixture into the air fryer baking dish.
4. Place in the air fryer and cook at 370 F for 25 minutes.
5. Serve and enjoy.

Nutritional Value (Amount per Serving):

- Calories 122
- Fat 8.8 g
- Carbohydrates 10.6 g
- Sugar 4.8 g
- Protein 1.3 g
- Cholesterol 23 mg

Daikon Chips

Preparation Time: 10 minutes
Cooking Time: 16 minutes
Serve: 6

Ingredients:

- 15 oz Daikon, slice into chips
- 1 tbsp olive oil
- 1 tsp chili powder
- 1/2 tsp pepper
- 1 tsp salt

Directions:

1. Preheat the air fryer to 375 F.
2. Add all ingredients into the bowl and toss to coat.
3. Transfer sliced the daikon into the air fryer basket and cook for 16 minutes. Toss halfway through.
4. Serve and enjoy.

Nutritional Value (Amount per Serving):

- Calories 36
- Fat 2.4 g
- Carbohydrates 3.2 g
- Sugar 1.5 g
- Protein 1.5 g
- Cholesterol 0 mg

Spicy Dip

Preparation Time: 5 minutes
Cooking Time: 5 minutes
Serve: 6

Ingredients:

- 12 oz hot peppers, chopped
- 1 1/2 cups apple cider vinegar
- Pepper
- Salt

Directions:

1. Add all ingredients into the air fryer baking dish and stir well.
2. Place dish in the air fryer and cook at 380 F for 5 minutes.
3. Transfer pepper mixture into the blender and blend until smooth.
4. Serve and enjoy.

Nutritional Value (Amount per Serving):

- Calories 35
- Fat 0.3 g
- Carbohydrates 5.6 g
- Sugar 3.3 g
- Protein 1.1 g
- Cholesterol 0 mg

Parmesan Turnip Slices

Preparation Time: 10 minutes
Cooking Time: 10 minutes
Serve: 8

Ingredients:

- 1 lb turnip, peel and cut into slices
- 1 tbsp olive oil
- 3 oz parmesan cheese, shredded
- 1 tsp garlic powder
- 1 tsp salt

Directions:

1. Preheat the air fryer to 360 F.
2. Add all ingredients into the mixing bowl and toss to coat.
3. Transfer turnip slices into the air fryer basket and cook for 10 minutes.
4. Serve and enjoy.

Nutritional Value (Amount per Serving):

- Calories 66
- Fat 4.1 g
- Carbohydrates 4.3 g
- Sugar 2.2 g
- Protein 4 g
- Cholesterol 8 mg

Perfect Crab Dip

Preparation Time: 5 minutes
Cooking Time: 7 minutes
Serve:4

Ingredients:

- 1 cup crabmeat
- 2 tbsp parsley, chopped
- 2 tbsp fresh lemon juice
- 2 tbsp hot sauce
- 1/2 cup green onion, sliced
- 2 cups cheese, grated
- 1/4 cup mayonnaise
- 1/4 tsp pepper
- 1/2 tsp salt

Directions:

1. In a 6-inch dish, mix together crabmeat, hot sauce, cheese, mayo, pepper, and salt.
2. Place dish in air fryer basket and cook dip at 400 F for 7 minutes.
3. Remove dish from air fryer.
4. Drizzle dip with lemon juice and garnish with parsley.
5. Serve and enjoy.

Nutritional Value (Amount per Serving):

- Calories 313
- Fat 23.9 g
- Carbohydrates 8.8 g
- Sugar 3.1 g
- Protein 16.2 g
- Cholesterol 67 mg

Kohlrabi Chips

Preparation Time: 10 minutes
Cooking Time: 20 minutes
Serve: 10

Ingredients:

- 1 lb kohlrabi, peel and slice thinly
- 1 tsp paprika
- 1 tbsp olive oil
- 1 tsp salt

Directions:

1. Preheat the air fryer to 320 F.
2. Add all ingredients into the bowl and toss to coat.
3. Transfer kohlrabi into the air fryer basket and cook for 20 minutes. Toss halfway through.
4. Serve and enjoy.

Nutritional Value (Amount per Serving):

- Calories 13
- Fat 1.4 g
- Carbohydrates 0.1 g
- Sugar 0 g
- Protein 0 g
- Cholesterol 0 mg

Flavorful Pork Meatballs

Preparation Time: 10 minutes
Cooking Time: 10 minutes
Serve: 4

Ingredients:

- 2 eggs, lightly beaten
- 2 tbsp capers
- 1/2 lb ground pork
- 3 garlic cloves, minced
- 2 tbsp fresh mint, chopped
- 1/2 tbsp cilantro, chopped
- 2 tsp red pepper flakes, crushed
- 1 1/2 tbsp butter, melted
- 1 tsp kosher salt

Directions:

1. Preheat the air fryer to 395 F.
2. Add all ingredients into the mixing bowl and mix until well combined.
3. Spray air fryer basket with cooking spray.
4. Make small balls from meat mixture and place into the air fryer basket.
5. Cook meatballs for 10 minutes. Shake basket halfway through.
6. Serve and enjoy.

Nutritional Value (Amount per Serving):

- Calories 159
- Fat 8.7 g
- Carbohydrates 1.9 g
- Sugar 0.3 g
- Protein 18.1 g
- Cholesterol 135 mg

Bacon Jalapeno Poppers

Preparation Time: 10 minutes
Cooking Time: 8 minutes
Serve: 10

Ingredients:

- 10 jalapeno peppers, cut in half and remove seeds
- 1/3 cup cream cheese, softened
- 5 bacon strips, cut in half

Directions:

1. Preheat the air fryer to 370 F.
2. Stuff cream cheese into each jalapeno half.
3. Wrap each jalapeno half with half bacon strip and place in the air fryer basket.
4. Cook for 6-8 minutes.
5. Serve and enjoy.

Nutritional Value (Amount per Serving):

- Calories 83
- Fat 7.4 g
- Carbohydrates 1.3 g
- Sugar 0.5 g
- Protein 2.8 g
- Cholesterol 9 mg

Veggie Cream Stuff Mushrooms

Preparation Time: 10 minutes
Cooking Time: 8 minutes
Serve: 12

Ingredients:

- 24 oz mushrooms, cut stems
- 1/2 cup sour cream
- 1 cup cheddar cheese, shredded
- 1 small carrot, diced
- 1/2 bell pepper, diced
- 1/2 onion, diced
- 2 bacon slices, diced

Directions:

1. Chop mushroom stems finely.
2. Spray pan with cooking spray and heat over medium heat.
3. Add chopped mushrooms, bacon, carrot, onion, and bell pepper into the pan and cook until tender.
4. Remove pan from heat. Add cheese and sour cream into the cooked vegetables and stir well.
5. Stuff vegetable mixture into the mushroom cap and place into the air fryer basket.
6. Cook mushrooms at 350 F for 8 minutes.
7. Serve and enjoy.

Nutritional Value (Amount per Serving):

- Calories 93
- Fat 6.6 g
- Carbohydrates 3.7 g
- Sugar 1.7 g
- Protein 5.7 g
- Cholesterol 18 mg

Chapter 3: Brunch Recipes

Lemon Dill Scallops

Preparation Time: 10 minutes

Cooking Time: 5 minutes

Serve: 4

Ingredients:

- 1 lb scallops
- 2 tsp olive oil
- 1 tsp dill, chopped
- 1 tbsp fresh lemon juice
- Pepper
- Salt

Directions:

1. Add scallops into the bowl and toss with oil, dill, lemon juice, pepper, and salt.
2. Add scallops into the air fryer basket and cook at 360 F for 5 minutes.
3. Serve and enjoy.

Nutritional Value (Amount per Serving):

- Calories 121
- Fat 3.2 g
- Carbohydrates 2.9 g
- Sugar 0.1 g
- Protein 19 g
- Cholesterol 37 mg

Zucchini Cheese Quiche

Preparation Time: 10 minutes
Cooking Time: 35 minutes
Serve: 6

Ingredients:

- 8 eggs
- 1 cup zucchini, shredded and squeezed
- 1 cup ham, cooked and diced
- 1/2 tsp dry mustard
- 1/2 cup heavy cream
- 1 cup cheddar cheese, shredded
- Pepper
- Salt

Directions:

1. Preheat the air fryer to 350 F.
2. Spray air fryer baking dish with cooking spray.
3. Combine ham, cheddar cheese, and zucchini in a baking dish.
4. In a bowl, whisk together eggs, heavy cream, and seasoning. Pour egg mixture over ham mixture.
5. Place dish in the air fryer and cook for 30-35 minutes.
6. Serve and enjoy.

Nutritional Value (Amount per Serving):

- Calories 234
- Fat 17 g
- Carbohydrates 2.5 g
- Sugar 1 g
- Protein 16 g
- Cholesterol 265 mg

Vegetable Egg Cups

Preparation Time:10 minutes
Cooking Time:20 minutes
Serve:4

Ingredients:

- 4 eggs
- 1 tbsp cilantro, chopped
- 4 tbsp half and half
- 1 cup cheddar cheese, shredded
- 1 cup vegetables, diced
- Pepper
- Salt

Directions:

1. Spray four ramekins with cooking spray and set aside.
2. In a mixing bowl, whisk eggs with cilantro, half and half, vegetables, 1/2 cup cheese, pepper, and salt.
3. Pour egg mixture into the four ramekins.
4. Place ramekins in air fryer basket and cook at 300 F for 12 minutes.
5. Top with remaining 1/2 cup cheese and cook for 2 minutes more at 400 F.
6. Serve and enjoy.

Nutritional Value (Amount per Serving):

- Calories 194
- Fat 11.5 g
- Carbohydrates 6 g
- Sugar 0.5 g
- Protein 13 g
- Cholesterol 190 mg

Egg Muffins

Preparation Time: 10 minutes
Cooking Time: 15 minutes
Serve: 12

Ingredients:

- 9 eggs
- 1/2 cup onion, sliced
- 1 tbsp olive oil
- 8 oz ground sausage
- 1/4 cup coconut milk
- 1/2 tsp oregano
- 1 1/2 cups spinach
- 3/4 cup bell peppers, chopped
- Pepper
- Salt

Directions:

1. Preheat the air fryer to 325 F.
2. Add ground sausage in a pan and sauté over medium heat for 5 minutes.
3. Add olive oil, oregano, bell pepper, and onion and sauté until onion is translucent.
4. Add spinach to the pan and cook for 30 seconds.
5. Remove pan from heat and set aside.
6. In a mixing bowl, whisk together eggs, coconut milk, pepper, and salt until well beaten.
7. Add sausage and vegetable mixture into the egg mixture and mix well.
8. Pour egg mixture into the silicone muffin molds and place into the air fryer basket. (Cook in batches)
9. Cook muffins for 15 minutes.
10. Serve and enjoy.

Nutritional Value (Amount per Serving):

- Calories 135
- Fat 11 g
- Carbohydrates 1.5 g
- Sugar 1 g
- Protein 8 g
- Cholesterol 140 mg

Almond Crust Chicken

Preparation Time: 10 minutes
Cooking Time: 25 minutes
Serve: 2

Ingredients:

- 2 chicken breasts, skinless and boneless
- 1 tbsp Dijon mustard
- 2 tbsp mayonnaise
- ¼ cup almonds
- Pepper
- Salt

Directions:

1. Add almond into the food processor and process until finely ground. Transfer almonds on a plate and set aside.
2. Mix together mustard and mayonnaise and spread over chicken.
3. Coat chicken with almond and place into the air fryer basket and cook at 350 F for 25 minutes.
4. Serve and enjoy.

Nutritional Value (Amount per Serving):

- Calories 409
- Fat 22 g
- Carbohydrates 6 g
- Sugar 1.5 g
- Protein 45 g
- Cholesterol 134 mg

Almond Pesto Salmon

Preparation Time: 10 minutes
Cooking Time: 12 minutes
Serve: 2

Ingredients:

- 2 salmon fillets
- 2 tbsp butter, melted
- ¼ cup pesto
- ¼ cup almond, ground

Directions:

1. Mix together pesto and almond.
2. Brush salmon fillets with melted butter and place into the air fryer baking dish.
3. Top salmon fillets with pesto and almond mixture.
4. Place dish in the air fryer and cook at 390 F for 12 minutes.
5. Serve and enjoy.

Nutritional Value (Amount per Serving):

- Calories 541
- Fat 41 g
- Carbohydrates 4 g
- Sugar 2.5 g
- Protein 40 g
- Cholesterol 117 mg

Spinach Frittata

Preparation Time: 5 minutes
Cooking Time: 8 minutes
Serve: 1

Ingredients:

- 3 eggs
- 1 cup spinach, chopped
- 1 small onion, minced
- 2 tbsp mozzarella cheese, grated
- Pepper
- Salt

Directions:

1. Preheat the air fryer to 350 F.
2. Spray air fryer pan with cooking spray.
3. In a bowl, whisk eggs with remaining ingredients until well combined.
4. Pour egg mixture into the prepared pan and place pan in the air fryer basket.
5. Cook frittata for 8 minutes or until set.
6. Serve and enjoy.

Nutritional Value (Amount per Serving):

- Calories 384
- Fat 23.3 g
- Carbohydrates 10.7 g
- Sugar 4.1 g
- Protein 34.3 g
- Cholesterol 521 mg

Zucchini Squash Mix

Preparation Time: 10 minutes
Cooking Time: 35 minutes
Serve: 4

Ingredients:

- 1 lb zucchini, sliced
- 1 tbsp parsley, chopped
- 1 yellow squash, halved, deseeded, and chopped
- 1 tbsp olive oil
- Pepper
- Salt

Directions:

1. Add all ingredients into the large bowl and mix well.
2. Transfer bowl mixture into the air fryer basket and cook at 400 F for 35 minutes.
3. Serve and enjoy.

Nutritional Value (Amount per Serving):

- Calories 49
- Fat 3 g
- Carbohydrates 4 g
- Sugar 2 g
- Protein 1.5 g
- Cholesterol 0 mg

Radish Hash Browns

Preparation Time: 10 minutes

Cooking Time: 13 minutes

Serve: 4

Ingredients:

- 1 lb radishes, washed and cut off roots
- 1 tbsp olive oil
- 1/2 tsp paprika
- 1/2 tsp onion powder
- 1/2 tsp garlic powder
- 1 medium onion
- 1/4 tsp pepper
- 3/4 tsp sea salt

Directions:

1. Slice onion and radishes using a mandolin slicer.
2. Add sliced onion and radishes in a large mixing bowl and toss with olive oil.
3. Transfer onion and radish slices in air fryer basket and cook at 360 F for 8 minutes. Shake basket twice.
4. Return onion and radish slices in a mixing bowl and toss with seasonings.
5. Again, cook onion and radish slices in air fryer basket for 5 minutes at 400 F. Shake basket halfway through.
6. Serve and enjoy.

Nutritional Value (Amount per Serving):

- Calories 62
- Fat 3.7 g
- Carbohydrates 7.1 g
- Sugar 3.5 g
- Protein 1.2 g
- Cholesterol 0 mg

Breakfast Casserole

Preparation Time: 10 minutes
Cooking Time: 28 minutes
Serve: 4

Ingredients:

- 2 eggs
- 4 egg whites
- 4 tsp pine nuts, minced
- 2/3 cup chicken broth
- 1 lb Italian sausage
- 1/4 cup roasted red pepper, sliced
- 1/4 cup pesto sauce
- 2/3 cup parmesan cheese, grated
- 1/8 tsp pepper
- 1/4 tsp sea salt

Directions:

1. Preheat the air fryer to 370 F.
2. Spray air fryer pan with cooking spray and set aside.
3. Heat another pan over medium heat. Add sausage in a pan and cook until golden brown.
4. Once cooked then drain excess oil and spread it into the prepared pan.
5. Whisk remaining ingredients except pine nuts in a bowl and pour over sausage.
6. Place pan in the air fryer and cook for 25-28 minutes.
7. Top with pine nuts and serve.

Nutritional Value (Amount per Serving):

- Calories 625
- Fat 49 g
- Carbohydrates 2 g
- Sugar 2.1 g
- Protein 39 g
- Cholesterol 200 mg

Shrimp Stuff Peppers

Preparation Time: 10 minutes
Cooking Time: 6 minutes
Serve: 6

Ingredients:

- 12 baby bell peppers, cut into halves
- 1 tbsp olive oil
- 1 tbsp fresh lemon juice
- ¼ cup basil pesto
- 1 lb shrimp, cooked
- ½ tsp red pepper flakes, crushed
- 2 tbsp parsley, chopped
- Pepper
- Salt

Directions:

1. In a bowl, mix together shrimp, parsley, red pepper flakes, basil pesto, lemon juice, oil, pepper, and salt.
2. Stuff shrimp mixture into the bell pepper halved and place into the air fryer basket.
3. Cook at 320 F for 6 minutes.
4. Serve and enjoy.

Nutritional Value (Amount per Serving):

- Calories 191
- Fat 3.7 g
- Carbohydrates 13 g
- Sugar 12 g
- Protein 19 g
- Cholesterol 159 mg

Chicken Meatballs

Preparation Time: 10 minutes
Cooking Time: 12 minutes
Serve: 4

Ingredients:

- 1 lb ground chicken
- 1/3 cup frozen spinach, drained and thawed
- 1/3 cup feta cheese, crumbled
- 1 tsp greek seasoning
- ½ oz pork rinds, crushed
- Pepper
- Salt

Directions:

1. Spray air fryer basket with cooking spray.
2. Add all ingredients into the large bowl and mix until well combined.
3. Make small balls from meat mixture and place into the air fryer basket and cook for 12 minutes.
4. Serve and enjoy.

Nutritional Value (Amount per Serving):

- Calories 271
- Fat 12 g
- Carbohydrates 1 g
- Sugar 0.5 g
- Protein 37 g
- Cholesterol 117 mg

Crab Cheese Frittata

Preparation Time: 10 minutes
Cooking Time: 14 minutes
Serve: 2

Ingredients:

- 5 eggs
- ¼ tsp fresh lemon juice
- 2 tbsp fresh mint, chopped
- 1/3 cup goat cheese, crumbled
- ¼ cup onion, minced
- ¼ tsp pepper
- ¼ tsp salt

Directions:

1. Preheat the air fryer to 325 F.
2. In a bowl, whisk eggs with pepper and salt. Add remaining ingredients and stir well.
3. Spray air fryer baking dish with cooking spray.
4. Pour egg mixture into the prepared dish and place in the air fryer and cook for 14 minutes.
5. Serve and enjoy.

Nutritional Value (Amount per Serving):

- Calories 325
- Fat 25 g
- Carbohydrates 2.9 g
- Sugar 1.5 g
- Protein 24 g
- Cholesterol 469 mg

Chapter 4: Poultry Recipes

Delicious Whole Chicken

Preparation Time: 10 minutes

Cooking Time: 50 minutes

Serve: 4

Ingredients:

- 3 lbs whole chicken, remove giblets and pat dry chicken
- 1 tsp Italian seasoning
- 1/2 tsp garlic powder
- 1/2 tsp onion powder
- 1/4 tsp paprika
- 1/4 tsp pepper
- 1 1/2 tsp salt

Directions:

1. In a small bowl, mix together Italian seasoning, garlic powder, onion powder, paprika, pepper, and salt.
2. Rub spice mixture from inside and outside of the chicken.
3. Place chicken breast side down in air fryer basket.
4. Roast chicken for 30 minutes at 360 F.
5. Turn chicken and roast for 20 minutes more or internal temperature of chicken reaches at 165 F.
6. Serve and enjoy.

Nutritional Value (Amount per Serving):

- Calories 356
- Fat 25 g
- Carbohydrates 1 g
- Sugar 1 g
- Protein 30 g
- Cholesterol 120 mg

Yummy Chicken Nuggets

Preparation Time: 10 minutes
Cooking Time: 12 minutes
Serve: 4

Ingredients:

- 1 lb chicken breast, skinless, boneless and cut into chunks
- 6 tbsp sesame seeds, toasted
- 4 egg whites
- 1/2 tsp ground ginger
- 1/4 cup coconut flour
- 1 tsp sesame oil
- Pinch of salt

Directions:

1. Preheat the air fryer to 400 F.
2. Toss chicken with oil and salt in a bowl until well coated.
3. Add coconut flour and ginger in a zip-lock bag and shake to mix. Add chicken to the bag and shake well to coat.
4. In a large bowl, add egg whites. Add chicken in egg whites and toss until well coated.
5. Add sesame seeds in a large zip-lock bag.
6. Shake excess egg off from chicken and add chicken in sesame seed bag. Shake bag until chicken well coated with sesame seeds.
7. Spray air fryer basket with cooking spray.
8. Place chicken in air fryer basket and cook for 6 minutes.
9. Turn chicken to another side and cook for 6 minutes more.
10. Serve and enjoy.

Nutritional Value (Amount per Serving):

- Calories 265
- Fat 11.5 g
- Carbohydrates 8.6 g
- Sugar 0.3 g
- Protein 31.1 g
- Cholesterol 73 mg

Chicken Kabab

Preparation Time: 10 minutes
Cooking Time: 6 minutes
Serve: 3

Ingredients:

- 1 lb ground chicken
- 1 tbsp fresh lemon juice
- ¼ cup almond flour
- 2 green onion, chopped
- 1 egg, lightly beaten
- 1/3 cup fresh parsley, chopped
- 3 garlic cloves
- 4 oz onion, chopped
- ¼ tsp turmeric powder
- ½ tsp pepper

Directions:

1. Add all ingredients into the food processor and process until well combined.
2. Transfer chicken mixture to the bowl and place in the refrigerator for 1 hour.
3. Divide mixture into the 6 equal portions and roll around the soaked wooden skewers.
4. Spray air fryer basket with cooking spray.
5. Place skewers into the air fryer basket and cooks at 400 F for 6 minutes.
6. Serve and enjoy.

Nutritional Value (Amount per Serving):

- Calories 290
- Fat 7 g
- Carbohydrates 6 g
- Sugar 2 g
- Protein 48 g
- Cholesterol 123 mg

Korean Chicken Tenders

Preparation Time: 10 minutes
Cooking Time: 10 minutes
Serve: 3

Ingredients:

- 12 oz chicken tenders, skinless and boneless
- 2 tbsp green onion, chopped
- 3 garlic cloves, chopped
- 2 tsp sesame seeds, toasted
- 1 tbsp ginger, grated
- 1/4 cup sesame oil
- 1/2 cup soy sauce
- 1/4 tsp pepper

Directions:

1. Slide chicken tenders onto the skewers.
2. In a large bowl, mix together green onion, garlic, sesame seeds, ginger, sesame oil, soy sauce, and pepper.
3. Add chicken skewers into the bowl and coat well with marinade. Place in refrigerator for overnight.
4. Preheat the air fryer to 390 F.
5. Place marinated chicken skewers into the air fryer basket and cook for 10 minutes.

Nutritional Value (Amount per Serving):

- Calories 423
- Fat 27 g
- Carbohydrates 6 g
- Sugar 1 g
- Protein 36 g
- Cholesterol 101 mg

Quick & Easy Meatballs

Preparation Time: 10 minutes
Cooking Time: 10 minutes
Serve: 4

Ingredients:

- 1 lb ground chicken
- 1 egg, lightly beaten
- 1/2 cup mozzarella cheese, shredded
- 1 1/2 tbsp taco seasoning
- 3 garlic cloves, minced
- 3 tbsp fresh parsley, chopped
- 1 small onion, minced
- Pepper
- Salt

Directions:

1. Add all ingredients into the large mixing bowl and mix until well combined.
2. Make small balls from mixture and place in the air fryer basket.
3. Cook meatballs for 10 minutes at 400 F.
4. Serve and enjoy.

Nutritional Value (Amount per Serving):

- Calories 253
- Fat 10 g
- Carbohydrates 2 g
- Sugar 0.9 g
- Protein 35 g
- Cholesterol 144 mg

Chicken Popcorn

Preparation Time: 10 minutes
Cooking Time: 10 minutes
Serve: 6

Ingredients:

- 4 eggs
- 1 1/2 lbs chicken breasts, cut into small chunks
- 1 tsp paprika
- 1/2 tsp garlic powder
- 1 tsp onion powder
- 2 1/2 cups pork rind, crushed
- 1/4 cup coconut flour
- Pepper
- Salt

Directions:

1. In a small bowl, mix together coconut flour, pepper, and salt.
2. In another bowl, whisk eggs until combined.
3. Take one more bowl and mix together pork panko, paprika, garlic powder, and onion powder.
4. Add chicken pieces in a large mixing bowl. Sprinkle coconut flour mixture over chicken and toss well.
5. Dip chicken pieces in the egg mixture and coat with pork panko mixture and place on a plate.
6. Spray air fryer basket with cooking spray.
7. Preheat the air fryer to 400 F.
8. Add half prepared chicken in air fryer basket and cook for 10-12 minutes. Shake basket halfway through.
9. Cook remaining half using the same method.
10. Serve and enjoy.

Nutritional Value (Amount per Serving):

- Calories 265
- Fat 11 g
- Carbohydrates 3 g
- Sugar 0.5 g
- Protein 35 g
- Cholesterol 195 mg

Flavorful Fried Chicken

Preparation Time: 10 minutes
Cooking Time: 40 minutes
Serve: 10

Ingredients:

- 5 lbs chicken, about 10 pieces
- 1 tbsp coconut oil
- 2 1/2 tsp white pepper
- 1 tsp ground ginger
- 1 1/2 tsp garlic salt
- 1 tbsp paprika
- 1 tsp dried mustard
- 1 tsp pepper
- 1 tsp celery salt
- 1/3 tsp oregano
- 1/2 tsp basil
- 1/2 tsp thyme
- 2 cups pork rinds, crushed
- 1 tbsp vinegar
- 1 cup unsweetened almond milk
- 1/2 tsp salt

Directions:

1. Add chicken in a large mixing bowl.
2. Add milk and vinegar over chicken and place in the refrigerator for 2 hours.
3. I a shallow dish, mix together pork rinds, white pepper, ginger, garlic salt, paprika, mustard, pepper, celery salt, oregano, basil, thyme, and salt.
4. Coat air fryer basket with coconut oil.
5. Coat each chicken piece with pork rind mixture and place on a plate.
6. Place half coated chicken in the air fryer basket.
7. Cook chicken at 360 F for 10 minutes then turn chicken to another side and cook for 10 minutes more or until internal temperature reaches at 165 F.
8. Cook remaining chicken using the same method.
9. Serve and enjoy.

Nutritional Value (Amount per Serving):

- Calories 539
- Fat 37 g
- Carbohydrates 1 g
- Sugar 0 g
- Protein 45 g
- Cholesterol 175 mg

Juicy Turkey Breast Tenderloin

Preparation Time: 10 minutes
Cooking Time: 25 minutes
Serve: 3

Ingredients:

- 1 turkey breast tenderloin
- 1/2 tsp sage
- 1/2 tsp smoked paprika
- 1/2 tsp pepper
- 1/2 tsp thyme
- 1/2 tsp salt

Directions:

1. Preheat the air fryer to 350 F.
2. Spray air fryer basket with cooking spray.
3. Rub turkey breast tenderloin with paprika, pepper, thyme, sage, and salt and place in the air fryer basket.
4. Cook for 25 minutes. Turn halfway through.
5. Slice and serve.

Nutritional Value (Amount per Serving):

- Calories 61
- Fat 1 g
- Carbohydrates 1 g
- Sugar 1 g
- Protein 12 g
- Cholesterol 25 mg

Tasty Southwest Chicken

Preparation Time: 10 minutes
Cooking Time: 25 minutes
Serve: 2

Ingredients:

- 1/2 lb chicken breasts, skinless and boneless
- 1/2 tsp chili powder
- 1 tbsp olive oil
- 1 tbsp lime juice
- 1/8 tsp garlic powder
- 1/8 tsp onion powder
- 1/4 tsp cumin
- 1/8 tsp salt

Directions:

1. Add all ingredients into the zip-lock bag and shake well to coat and place in the refrigerator for 1 hour.
2. Add a marinated chicken wing to the air fryer basket and cook at 400 F for 25 minutes. Shake halfway through.
3. Serve and enjoy.

Nutritional Value (Amount per Serving):

- Calories 250
- Fat 12 g
- Carbohydrates 0.6 g
- Sugar 0.1 g
- Protein 33 g
- Cholesterol 100 mg

Dijon Turkey Drumstick

Preparation Time: 10 minutes
Cooking Time: 28 minutes
Serve: 2

Ingredients:

- 4 turkey drumsticks
- 1/3 tsp paprika
- 1/3 cup sherry wine
- 1/3 cup coconut milk
- 1/2 tbsp ginger, minced
- 2 tbsp Dijon mustard
- Pepper
- Salt

Directions:

1. Add all ingredients into the large bowl and stir to coat. Place in refrigerator for 2 hours.
2. Spray air fryer basket with cooking spray.
3. Place marinated turkey drumsticks into the air fryer basket and cook at 380 F for 28 minutes. Turn halfway through.
4. Serve and enjoy.

Nutritional Value (Amount per Serving):

- Calories 365
- Fat 18 g
- Carbohydrates 5 g
- Sugar 2 g
- Protein 40 g
- Cholesterol 0 mg

Zaatar Chicken

Preparation Time: 10 minutes
Cooking Time: 35 minutes
Serve: 4

Ingredients:

- 4 chicken thighs
- 2 sprigs thyme
- 1 onion, cut into chunks
- 2 1/2 tbsp zaatar
- 1/2 tsp cinnamon
- 2 garlic cloves, smashed
- 1 lemon juice
- 1 lemon zest
- 1/4 cup olive oil
- 1/4 tsp pepper
- 1 tsp salt

Directions:

1. Add oil, lemon juice, lemon zest, cinnamon, garlic, pepper, 2 tbsp zaatar, and salt in a large zip-lock bag and shake well.
2. Add chicken, thyme, and onion to bag and shake well to coat. Place in refrigerator for overnight.
3. Preheat the air fryer to 380 F.
4. Add marinated chicken in air fryer basket and cook at 380 F for 15 minutes.
5. Turn chicken to another side and sprinkle with remaining za'atar spice and cook at 380 F for 15-18 minutes more.
6. Serve and enjoy.

Nutritional Value (Amount per Serving):

- Calories 415
- Fat 24.1 g
- Carbohydrates 5.2 g
- Sugar 1.5 g
- Protein 43 g
- Cholesterol 130 mg

Cilantro Lime Chicken

Preparation Time: 10 minutes
Cooking Time: 20 minutes
Serve: 4

Ingredients:

- 2 lbs chicken thighs, boneless
- 2 tbsp fresh cilantro, chopped
- 1 tsp Montreal chicken seasoning
- 1 tsp soy sauce
- 1/2 lime juice
- 1 tsp olive oil
- Pepper
- Salt

Directions:

1. Whisk together cilantro, seasoning, soy sauce, lime juice, olive oil, pepper, and salt in a large bowl.
2. Add chicken into the bowl and coat well with marinade and place in the refrigerator for overnight.
3. Spray air fryer basket with cooking spray.
4. Place marinated chicken into the air fryer basket and cook at 400 F for 10 minutes.
5. Turn chicken to another side and cook for 10 minutes more.
6. Serve and enjoy.

Nutritional Value (Amount per Serving):

- Calories 444
- Fat 18 g
- Carbohydrates 0.8 g
- Sugar 0.1 g
- Protein 65.8 g
- Cholesterol 202 mg

Meatloaf

Preparation Time: 10 minutes
Cooking Time: 28 minutes
Serve: 8

Ingredients:

- 1 egg
- 1 tsp chili powder
- 1 tsp garlic powder
- 1 tsp garlic, minced
- 2 lbs ground turkey
- 2 oz BBQ sauce, sugar-free
- 1 tsp ground mustard
- 1 tbsp onion, minced
- 1 cup cheddar cheese, shredded
- 1 tsp salt

Directions:

1. Preheat the air fryer to 370 F.
2. In a large bowl, combine together all ingredients then transfer into the silicon loaf pan.
3. Place loaf pan in the air fryer and cook for 25-28 minutes.
4. Serve and enjoy.

Nutritional Value (Amount per Serving):

- Calories 301
- Fat 17 g
- Carbohydrates 3 g
- Sugar 2.2 g
- Protein 35.5 g
- Cholesterol 150 mg

Chapter 5: Beef Pork & Lamb Recipes

Vietnamese Pork Chop

Preparation Time: 10 minutes
Cooking Time: 15 minutes
Serve: 2

Ingredients:

- 2 pork chops
- 1 tbsp olive oil
- 1 tbsp soy sauce
- 1 tsp pepper
- 2 1/2 tbsp lemongrass, chopped
- 1 tbsp onion, chopped
- 3 garlic cloves, chopped

Directions:

1. Add all ingredients into the bowl and coat well. Place in refrigerator for 2 hours.
2. Preheat the air fryer to 400 F.
3. Place marinated pork chops into the air fryer and cook for 7 minutes.
4. Turn pork chops to another side and cook for 5 minutes more.
5. Serve and enjoy.

Nutritional Value (Amount per Serving):

- Calories 340
- Fat 28 g
- Carbohydrates 6 g
- Sugar 0.5 g
- Protein 20 g
- Cholesterol 70 mg

Cheesy & Juicy Pork Chops

Preparation Time: 10 minutes
Cooking Time: 8 minutes
Serve: 2

Ingredients:

- 4 pork chops
- 1/4 cup cheddar cheese, shredded
- 1/2 tsp garlic powder
- 1/2 tsp salt

Directions:

1. Preheat the air fryer to 350 F.
2. Rub pork chops with garlic powder and salt and place in the air fryer basket.
3. Cook pork chops for 4 minutes.
4. Turn pork chops to another side and cook for 2 minutes.
5. Add cheese on top of pork chops and cook for 2 minutes more.
6. Serve and enjoy.

Nutritional Value (Amount per Serving):

- Calories 465
- Fat 22 g
- Carbohydrates 2 g
- Sugar 0.6 g
- Protein 61 g
- Cholesterol 190 mg

Italian Sausage Meatballs

Preparation Time: 10 minutes
Cooking Time: 15 minutes
Serve: 8

Ingredients:

- 1 lb Italian sausage
- 1 lb ground beef
- 1/2 tsp Italian seasoning
- 1/2 tsp red pepper flakes
- 1 1/2 cups parmesan cheese, grated
- 2 egg, lightly beaten
- 2 tbsp parsley, chopped
- 2 garlic cloves, minced
- 1/4 cup onion, minced
- Pepper
- Salt

Directions:

1. Add all ingredients into the large mixing bowl and mix until well combined.
2. Spray air fryer basket with cooking spray.
3. Make meatballs from bowl mixture and place into the air fryer basket.
4. Cook at 350 F for 15 minutes.
5. Serve and enjoy.

Nutritional Value (Amount per Serving):

- Calories 334
- Fat 21.9 g
- Carbohydrates 1 g
- Sugar 0.3 g
- Protein 31.4 g
- Cholesterol 143 mg

Crisp Pork Chops

Preparation Time: 10 minutes
Cooking Time: 12 minutes
Serve: 6

Ingredients:

- 1 1/2 lbs pork chops, boneless
- 1 tsp paprika
- 1 tsp creole seasoning
- 1 tsp garlic powder
- 1/4 cup parmesan cheese, grated
- 1/3 cup almond flour

Directions:

1. Preheat the air fryer to 360 F.
2. Add all ingredients except pork chops in a zip-lock bag.
3. Add pork chops in the bag. Seal bag and shake well to coat pork chops.
4. Remove pork chops from zip-lock bag and place in the air fryer basket.
5. Cook pork chops for 10-12 minutes.
6. Serve and enjoy.

Nutritional Value (Amount per Serving):

- Calories 230
- Fat 11 g
- Carbohydrates 2 g
- Sugar 0.2 g
- Protein 27 g
- Cholesterol 79 mg

Parmesan Pork Chops

Preparation Time: 10 minutes
Cooking Time: 15 minutes
Serve: 4

Ingredients:

- 4 pork chops, boneless
- 4 tbsp parmesan cheese, grated
- 1 cup pork rind
- 2 eggs, lightly beaten
- 1/2 tsp chili powder
- 1/2 tsp onion powder
- 1 tsp paprika
- 1/4 tsp pepper
- 1/2 tsp salt

Directions:

1. Preheat the air fryer to 400 F.
2. Season pork chops with pepper and salt.
3. Add pork rind in food processor and process until crumbs form.
4. Mix together pork rind crumbs and seasoning in a large bowl.
5. Place egg in a separate bowl.
6. Dip pork chops in egg mixture then coat with pork crumb mixture and place in the air fryer basket.
7. Cook pork chops for 12-15 minutes.
8. Serve and enjoy.

Nutritional Value (Amount per Serving):

- Calories 329
- Fat 24 g
- Carbohydrates 1 g
- Sugar 0.4 g
- Protein 23 g
- Cholesterol 158 mg

Meatloaf Sliders

Preparation Time: 10 minutes
Cooking Time: 10 minutes
Serve: 8

Ingredients:

- 1 lb ground beef
- 1/2 tsp dried tarragon
- 1 tsp Italian seasoning
- 1 tbsp Worcestershire sauce
- 1/4 cup ketchup
- 1/4 cup coconut flour
- 1/2 cup almond flour
- 1 garlic clove, minced
- 1/4 cup onion, chopped
- 2 eggs, lightly beaten
- 1/4 tsp pepper
- 1/2 tsp sea salt

Directions:

1. Add all ingredients into the mixing bowl and mix until well combined.
2. Make the equal shape of patties from mixture and place on a plate. Place in refrigerator for 10 minutes.
3. Spray air fryer basket with cooking spray.
4. Preheat the air fryer to 360 F.
5. Place prepared patties in air fryer basket and cook for 10 minutes.
6. Serve and enjoy.

Nutritional Value (Amount per Serving):

- Calories 228
- Fat 16 g
- Carbohydrates 6 g
- Sugar 2 g
- Protein 13 g
- Cholesterol 80 mg

Easy Burger Patties

Preparation Time: 10 minutes
Cooking Time: 45 minutes
Serve: 4

Ingredients:

- 10 oz ground beef
- 1 tsp dried basil
- 1 tsp mustard
- 1 tsp tomato paste
- 1 oz cheddar cheese
- 1 tsp mixed herbs
- 1 tsp garlic puree
- Pepper
- Salt

Directions:

1. Add all ingredients into the large bowl and mix until combined.
2. Spray air fryer basket with cooking spray.
3. Make patties from meat mixture and place into the air fryer basket.
4. Cook at 390 F for 25 minutes then turn patties to another side and cook at 350 F for 20 minutes more.
5. Serve and enjoy.

Nutritional Value (Amount per Serving):

- Calories 175
- Fat 7 g
- Carbohydrates 1 g
- Sugar 2 g
- Protein 25 g
- Cholesterol 125 mg

Asian Beef

Preparation Time: 10 minutes
Cooking Time: 20 minutes
Serve: 4

Ingredients:

- 1 lb beef tips, sliced
- 1/4 cup green onion, chopped
- 2 tbsp garlic, minced
- 2 tbsp sesame oil
- 1 tbsp fish sauce
- 2 tbsp coconut aminos
- 1 tsp xanthan gum
- 2 red chili peppers, sliced
- 2 tbsp water
- 1 tbsp ginger, sliced

Directions:

1. Spray air fryer basket with cooking spray.
2. Toss beef and xanthan gum together.
3. Add beef into the air fryer basket and cook at 390F for 20 minutes. Toss halfway through.
4. Meanwhile, in a saucepan add remaining ingredients except for green onion and heat over low heat.
5. When sauce begins to boiling then remove from heat.
6. Add cooked meat into the saucepan and stir to coat. Let sit in for 5 minutes.
7. Garnish with green onion and serve.

Nutritional Value (Amount per Serving):

- Calories 295
- Fat 15 g
- Carbohydrates 6 g
- Sugar 0.4 g
- Protein 35 g
- Cholesterol 42 mg

Classic Pork

Preparation Time: 10 minutes
Cooking Time: 10 minutes
Serve: 4

Ingredients:

- 1 lb pork shoulder, thinly sliced
- 1 tbsp fish sauce
- 3 garlic cloves, minced
- 1 tbsp Swerve
- 2 tbsp olive oil
- 1/4 cup onion, minced
- 1/2 tsp pepper
- 1 tbsp lemongrass paste

Directions:

1. In a bowl, whisk together onion, pepper, lemongrass paste, fish sauce, garlic, sweetener, and oil.
2. Add meat slices into the bowl and coat well. Place in the fridge for 1 hour.
3. Place marinated meat in the air fryer basket and cook at 400 F for 10 minutes. Turn halfway through.
4. Serve and enjoy.

Nutritional Value (Amount per Serving):

- Calories 415
- Fat 32 g
- Carbohydrates 5 g
- Sugar 4 g
- Protein 27 g
- Cholesterol 105 mg

Meatloaf

Preparation Time: 10 minutes
Cooking Time: 15 minutes
Serve: 4

Ingredients:

- 1 lb ground beef
- 1/4 tsp cinnamon
- 1 tbsp ginger, minced
- 1/4 cup fresh cilantro, chopped
- 1 cup onion, diced
- 2 eggs, lightly beaten
- 1 tsp cayenne
- 1 tsp turmeric
- 1 tsp garam masala
- 1 tbsp garlic, minced
- 1 tsp salt

Directions:

1. Add all ingredients into the large bowl and mix until combined.
2. Transfer meat mixture into the silicone meatloaf pan.
3. Place in the air fryer and cook at 360 F for 15 minutes.
4. Slice and serve.

Nutritional Value (Amount per Serving):

- Calories 260
- Fat 10 g
- Carbohydrates 4 g
- Sugar 2 g
- Protein 38 g
- Cholesterol 25 mg

Delicious Burger

Preparation Time: 10 minutes
Cooking Time: 10 minutes
Serve: 2

Ingredients:

- 1/2 lb ground beef
- 1 tsp swerve
- 1 tsp ginger, minced
- 1/2 tbsp soy sauce
- 1 tbsp gochujang
- 1 tbsp green onion, chopped
- 1/2 tbsp sesame oil
- 1/4 tsp salt

Directions:

1. In a large bowl, mix together all ingredients until well combined. Place in refrigerator for 1 hour.
2. Make patties from beef mixture and place into the air fryer basket.
3. Cook at 360 F for 10 minutes.
4. Serve and enjoy.

Nutritional Value (Amount per Serving):

- Calories 324
- Fat 16 g
- Carbohydrates 6 g
- Sugar 3 g
- Protein 36 g
- Cholesterol 102 mg

Rosemary Beef Roast

Preparation Time: 10 minutes
Cooking Time: 45 minutes
Serve: 6

Ingredients:

- 2 lbs beef roast
- 1 tbsp olive oil
- 1 tsp rosemary
- 1 tsp thyme
- 1/4 tsp pepper
- 1 tsp salt

Directions:

1. Preheat the air fryer to 360 F.
2. Mix together oil, rosemary, thyme, pepper, and salt and rub over the meat.
3. Place meat in the air fryer and cook for 45 minutes.
4. Serve and enjoy.

Nutritional Value (Amount per Serving):

- Calories 300
- Fat 12 g
- Carbohydrates 0.5 g
- Sugar 0 g
- Protein 46 g
- Cholesterol 123 mg

Meatballs

Preparation Time: 10 minutes
Cooking Time: 20 minutes
Serve: 4

Ingredients:

- 1/2 lb ground beef
- 1/2 lb Italian sausage
- 1/2 cup cheddar cheese, shredded
- 1/3 tsp pepper
- 1/2 tsp garlic powder
- 1 tsp onion powder

Directions:

1. Spray air fryer basket with cooking spray.
2. Add all ingredients into the large bowl and mix until combined.
3. Make small balls from meat mixture and place in the air fryer basket.
4. Cook at 370 F for 15 minutes. Turn to another side and cook for 5 minutes more.
5. Serve and enjoy.

Nutritional Value (Amount per Serving):

- Calories 356
- Fat 25 g
- Carbohydrates 1 g
- Sugar 0.5 g
- Protein 32 g
- Cholesterol 158 mg

Chapter 6: Seafood & Fish Recipes

Tuna Patties

Preparation Time: 10 minutes
Cooking Time: 10 minutes
Serve: 2

Ingredients:

- 2 cans tuna
- 1/2 lemon juice
- 1/2 tsp onion powder
- 1 tsp garlic powder
- 1/2 tsp dried dill
- 1 1/2 tbsp mayonnaise
- 1 1/2 tbsp almond flour
- 1/4 tsp pepper
- 1/4 tsp salt

Directions:

1. Preheat the air fryer to 400 F.
2. Add all ingredients in a mixing bowl and mix until well combined.
3. Spray air fryer basket with cooking spray.
4. Make four patties from mixture and place in the air fryer basket.
5. Cook patties for 10 minutes at 400 F if you want crispier patties then cook for 3 minutes more.
6. Serve and enjoy.

Nutritional Value (Amount per Serving):

- Calories 414
- Fat 20.6 g
- Carbohydrates 5.6 g
- Sugar 1.3 g
- Protein 48.8 g
- Cholesterol 58 mg

Chili Garlic Shrimp

Preparation Time: 10 minutes
Cooking Time: 7 minutes
Serve: 4

Ingredients:

- 1 lb shrimp, peeled and deveined
- 1 tbsp olive oil
- 1 lemon, sliced
- 1 red chili pepper, sliced
- 1/2 tsp garlic powder
- Pepper
- Salt

Directions:

1. Preheat the air fryer to 400 F.
2. Spray air fryer basket with cooking spray.
3. Add all ingredients into the bowl and toss well.
4. Add shrimp into the air fryer basket and cook for 5 minutes. Shake basket twice.
5. Serve and enjoy.

Nutritional Value (Amount per Serving):

- Calories 170
- Fat 5 g
- Carbohydrates 3 g
- Sugar 0.5 g
- Protein 25 g
- Cholesterol 0 mg

Pesto Salmon

Preparation Time: 10 minutes
Cooking Time: 16 minutes
Serve: 2

Ingredients:

- 2 salmon fillets
- 1/4 cup parmesan cheese, grated
- For pesto:
- 1/4 cup pine nuts
- 1/4 cup olive oil
- 1 1/2 cups fresh basil leaves
- 2 garlic cloves, peeled and chopped
- 1/4 cup parmesan cheese, grated
- 1/2 tsp pepper
- 1/2 tsp salt

Directions:

1. Add all pesto ingredients to the blender and blend until smooth.
2. Preheat the air fryer to 370 F.
3. Spray air fryer basket with cooking spray.
4. Place salmon fillet into the air fryer basket and spread 2 tablespoons of the pesto on each salmon fillet.
5. Sprinkle grated cheese on top of the pesto.
6. Cook salmon for 16 minutes.
7. Serve and enjoy.

Nutritional Value (Amount per Serving):

- Calories 725
- Fat 57 g
- Carbohydrates 4 g
- Sugar 0.7 g
- Protein 49 g
- Cholesterol 108 mg

Crispy Fish Sticks

Preparation Time: 10 minutes
Cooking Time: 10 minutes
Serve: 4

Ingredients:

- 1 lb white fish, cut into pieces
- 3/4 tsp Cajun seasoning
- 1 1/2 cups pork rind, crushed
- 2 tbsp water
- 2 tbsp Dijon mustard
- 1/4 cup mayonnaise
- Pepper
- Salt

Directions:

1. Spray air fryer basket with cooking spray.
2. In a small bowl, whisk together mayonnaise, water, and mustard.
3. In a shallow bowl, mix together pork rind, pepper, Cajun seasoning, and salt.
4. Dip fish pieces in mayo mixture and coat with pork rind mixture and place in the air fryer basket.
5. Cook at 400 F for 5 minutes. Turn fish sticks to another side and cook for 5 minutes more.
6. Serve and enjoy.

Nutritional Value (Amount per Serving):

- Calories 397
- Fat 36.4 g
- Carbohydrates 4 g
- Sugar 1 g
- Protein 14.7 g
- Cholesterol 4 mg

Lemon Chili Salmon

Preparation Time: 10 minutes
Cooking Time: 17 minutes
Serve: 4

Ingredients:

- 2 lbs salmon fillet, skinless and boneless
- 2 lemon juice
- 1 orange juice
- 1 tbsp olive oil
- 1 bunch fresh dill
- 1 chili, sliced
- Pepper
- Salt

Directions:

1. Preheat the air fryer to 325 F.
2. Place salmon fillets in air fryer baking pan and drizzle with olive oil, lemon juice, and orange juice.
3. Sprinkle chili slices over salmon and season with pepper and salt.
4. Place pan in the air fryer and cook for 15-17 minutes.
5. Garnish with dill and serve.

Nutritional Value (Amount per Serving):

- Calories 339
- Fat 17.5 g
- Carbohydrates 2 g
- Sugar 2 g
- Protein 44 g
- Cholesterol 100 mg

Delicious Crab Cakes

Preparation Time: 10 minutes
Cooking Time: 10 minutes
Serve: 4

Ingredients:

- 8 oz crab meat
- 2 tbsp butter, melted
- 2 tsp Dijon mustard
- 1 tbsp mayonnaise
- 1 egg, lightly beaten
- 1/2 tsp old bay seasoning
- 1 green onion, sliced
- 2 tbsp parsley, chopped
- 1/4 cup almond flour
- 1/4 tsp pepper
- 1/2 tsp salt

Directions:

1. Add all ingredients except butter in a mixing bowl and mix until well combined.
2. Make four equal shapes of patties from mixture and place on parchment lined plate.
3. Place plate in the fridge for 30 minutes.
4. Spray air fryer basket with cooking spray.
5. Brush melted butter on both sides of crab patties.
6. Place crab patties in air fryer basket and cook for 10 minutes at 350 F.
7. Turn patties halfway through.
8. Serve and enjoy.

Nutritional Value (Amount per Serving):

- Calories 136
- Fat 12.6 g
- Carbohydrates 4.1 g
- Sugar 0.5 g
- Protein 10.3 g
- Cholesterol 88 mg

Cajun Shrimp

Preparation Time: 10 minutes
Cooking Time: 8 minutes
Serve: 4

Ingredients:

- 1 lb shrimp, peeled and deveined
- 1 lime, cut into wedges
- 1/2 tbsp chipotle chili in adobo, minced
- 1 tbsp Cajun seasoning
- 2 tbsp olive oil
- Pepper
- Salt

Directions:

1. Add all ingredients into the large bowl and toss well to coat. Place in the fridge for 1 hour.
2. Spray air fryer basket with cooking spray.
3. Add marinated shrimp into the air fryer basket and cook at 400 F for 8 minutes.
4. Serve and enjoy.

Nutritional Value (Amount per Serving):

- Calories 201
- Fat 9.1 g
- Carbohydrates 3.6 g
- Sugar 0.3 g
- Protein 26.1 g
- Cho10sterol 239 mg

Thai Shrimp

Preparation Time: 10 minutes
Cooking Time: 10 minutes
Serve: 4

Ingredients:

- 1 lb shrimp, peeled and deveined
- 1 tsp sesame seeds, toasted
- 2 garlic cloves, minced
- 2 tbsp soy sauce
- 2 tbsp Thai chili sauce
- 1 tbsp arrowroot powder
- 1 tbsp green onion, sliced
- 1/8 tsp ginger, minced

Directions:

1. Spray air fryer basket with cooking spray.
2. Toss shrimp with arrowroot powder and place into the air fryer basket.
3. Cook shrimp at 350 F for 5 minutes. Shake basket well and cook for 5 minutes more.
4. Meanwhile, in a bowl, mix together soy sauce, ginger, garlic, and chili sauce.
5. Add shrimp to the bowl and toss well.
6. Garnish with green onions and sesame seeds.
7. Serve and enjoy.

Nutritional Value (Amount per Serving):

- Calories 155
- Fat 2 g
- Carbohydrates 6 g
- Sugar 2 g
- Protein 25 g
- Cholesterol 0 mg

Garlic Mayo Shrimp

Preparation Time: 10 minutes
Cooking Time: 8 minutes
Serve: 2

Ingredients:

- 1/2 lb shrimp, peeled
- 1/2 tbsp ketchup
- 1 1/2 tbsp mayonnaise
- 1/4 tsp paprika
- 1/2 tsp sriracha
- 1/2 tbsp garlic, minced
- 1/4 tsp salt

Directions:

1. In a bowl, mix together mayonnaise, paprika, sriracha, garlic, ketchup, and salt.
2. Add shrimp into the bowl and coat well.
3. Spray air fryer basket with cooking spray.
4. Transfer shrimp into the air fryer basket and cook at 325 F for 8 minutes. Shake halfway through.
5. Serve and enjoy.

Nutritional Value (Amount per Serving):

- Calories 185
- Fat 5.7 g
- Carbohydrates 6 g
- Sugar 1.6 g
- Protein 25 g
- Cholesterol 240 mg

Simple Salmon Patties

Preparation Time: 10 minutes
Cooking Time: 10 minutes
Serve: 2

Ingredients:

- 14 oz salmon
- 1/2 onion, diced
- 1 egg, lightly beaten
- 1 tsp dill
- 1/2 cup almond flour

Directions:

1. Spray air fryer basket with cooking spray.
2. Add all ingredients into the bowl and mix until well combined.
3. Spray air fryer basket with cooking spray.
4. Make patties from salmon mixture and place into the air fryer basket.
5. Cook at 370 F for 5 minutes.
6. Turn patties to another side and cook for 5 minutes more.
7. Serve and enjoy.

Nutritional Value (Amount per Serving):

- Calories 350
- Fat 15 g
- Carbohydrates 3 g
- Sugar 1 g
- Protein 44 g
- Cholesterol 0 mg

Air Fried King Prawns

Preparation Time: 10 minutes
Cooking Time: 6 minutes
Serve: 4

Ingredients:

- 12 king prawns
- 1 tbsp vinegar
- 1 tbsp ketchup
- 3 tbsp mayonnaise
- 1/2 tsp pepper
- 1 tsp chili powder
- 1 tsp red chili flakes
- 1/2 tsp sea salt

Directions:

1. Preheat the air fryer to 350 F.
2. Spray air fryer basket with cooking spray.
3. Add prawns, chili flakes, chili powder, pepper, and salt to the bowl and toss well.
4. Transfer shrimp to the air fryer basket and cook for 6 minutes.
5. In a small bowl, mix together mayonnaise, ketchup, and vinegar.
6. Serve with mayo mixture and enjoy.

Nutritional Value (Amount per Serving):

- Calories 130
- Fat 5 g
- Carbohydrates 5 g
- Sugar 1 g
- Protein 15 g
- Cholesterol 0 mg

Almond Coconut Shrimp

Preparation Time: 10 minutes
Cooking Time: 5 minutes
Serve: 4

Ingredients:

- 16 oz shrimp, peeled
- 1/2 cup almond flour
- 2 egg whites
- 1/4 tsp cayenne pepper
- 1/2 cup unsweetened shredded coconut
- 1/2 tsp salt

Directions:

1. Preheat the air fryer to 400 F.
2. Spray air fryer basket with cooking spray.
3. Whisk egg whites in a shallow dish.
4. In a bowl, mix together the shredded coconut, almond flour, and cayenne pepper.
5. Dip shrimp into the egg mixture then coat with coconut mixture.
6. Place coated shrimp into the air fryer basket and cook for 5 minutes.
7. Serve and enjoy.

Nutritional Value (Amount per Serving):

- Calories 200
- Fat 7 g
- Carbohydrates 4 g
- Sugar 1 g
- Protein 28 g
- Cholesterol 0 mg

Creamy Shrimp

Preparation Time: 10 minutes
Cooking Time: 8 minutes
Serve: 4

Ingredients:

- 1 lb shrimp, peeled
- 1 tbsp garlic, minced
- 1 tbsp tomato ketchup
- 3 tbsp mayonnaise
- 1/2 tsp paprika
- 1 tsp sriracha
- 1/2 tsp salt

Directions:

1. In a bowl, mix together mayonnaise, paprika, sriracha, garlic, ketchup, and salt. Add shrimp and stir well.
2. Add shrimp mixture into the air fryer baking dish and place in the air fryer.
3. Cook at 325 F for 8 minutes. Stir halfway through.
4. Serve and enjoy.

Nutritional Value (Amount per Serving):

- Calories 185
- Fat 5 g
- Carbohydrates 6 g
- Sugar 1 g
- Protein 25 g
- Cholesterol 0 mg

Chapter 7: Meatless Meals Recipes

Mushroom Bean Casserole

Preparation Time: 10 minutes

Cooking Time: 12 minutes

Serve: 6

Ingredients:

- 2 cups mushrooms, sliced
- 1 tsp onion powder
- 1/2 tsp ground sage
- 1/2 tbsp garlic powder
- 1 fresh lemon juice
- 1 1/2 lbs green beans, trimmed
- 1/4 tsp pepper
- 1/2 tsp salt

Directions:

1. In a large mixing bowl, toss together green beans, onion powder, sage, garlic powder, lemon juice, mushrooms, pepper, and salt.
2. Spray air fryer basket with cooking spray.
3. Transfer green bean mixture into the air fryer basket.
4. Cook for 10-12 minutes at 400 F. Shake after every 3 minutes.
5. Serve and enjoy.

Nutritional Value (Amount per Serving):

- Calories 45
- Fat 0.2 g
- Carbohydrates 9.8 g
- Sugar 2.3g
- Protein 3 g
- Cholesterol 0 mg

Garlic Thyme Mushrooms

Preparation Time: 10 minutes
Cooking Time: 23 minutes
Serve: 2

Ingredients:

- 10 oz mushrooms, quartered
- 1 tsp thyme, chopped
- 2 tbsp olive oil
- 2 garlic cloves, sliced
- 1/4 tsp pepper
- 1/4 tsp salt

Directions:

1. Preheat the air fryer to 370 F.
2. Spray air fryer basket with cooking spray.
3. In a bowl, combine together mushrooms, pepper, salt, thyme, and oil.
4. Spread mushrooms into the air fryer basket and cook for 20 minutes. Shake basket halfway through.
5. Add garlic and stir well and cook for 2-3 minutes.
6. Serve and enjoy.

Nutritional Value (Amount per Serving):

- Calories 155
- Fat 14.5 g
- Carbohydrates 6 g
- Sugar 2.5 g
- Protein 5 g
- Cholesterol 0 mg

Air Fried Onion & Bell Peppers

Preparation Time: 10 minutes
Cooking Time: 25 minutes
Serve: 3

Ingredients:

- 6 bell pepper, sliced
- 1 tbsp Italian seasoning
- 1 tbsp olive oil
- 1 onion, sliced

Directions:

1. Add all ingredients into the large mixing bowl and toss well.
2. Preheat the air fryer to 320 F.
3. Transfer bell pepper and onion mixture into the air fryer basket and cook for 15 minutes.
4. Toss well and cook for 10 minutes more.
5. Serve and enjoy.

Nutritional Value (Amount per Serving):

- Calories 129
- Fat 6.1g
- Carbohydrates 14 g
- Sugar 10 g
- Protein 3 g
- Cholesterol 3 mg

Asian Broccoli

Preparation Time: 10 minutes
Cooking Time: 20 minutes
Serve: 4

Ingredients:

- 1 lb broccoli, cut into florets
- 1 tsp rice vinegar
- 2 tsp sriracha
- 2 tbsp soy sauce
- 1 tbsp garlic, minced
- 5 drops liquid stevia
- 1 1/2 tbsp sesame oil
- Salt

Directions:

1. In a bowl, toss together broccoli, garlic, oil, and salt.
2. Spread broccoli in air fryer basket and cook for 15-20 minutes at 400 F.
3. Meanwhile, in a microwave-safe bowl mix together soy sauce, vinegar, liquid stevia, and sriracha and microwave for 10 seconds.
4. Transfer broccoli to a bowl and toss well with soy mixture to coat.
5. Serve and enjoy.

Nutritional Value (Amount per Serving):

- Calories 94
- Fat 5.5 g
- Carbohydrates 9.3 g
- Sugar 2.1 g
- Protein 3.8 g
- Cholesterol 0 mg

Parmesan Broccoli

Preparation Time: 10 minutes
Cooking Time: 5 minutes
Serve: 2

Ingredients:

- 3 cups broccoli florets
- 1/4 cup parmesan cheese, grated
- 2 tbsp olive oil
- 2 garlic cloves, minced

Directions:

1. Preheat the air fryer to 360 F.
2. Add all ingredients into the large bowl and toss well.
3. Transfer broccoli mixture into the air fryer basket and cook for 4-5 minutes.
4. Serve and enjoy.

Nutritional Value (Amount per Serving):

- Calories 182
- Fat 15.2 g
- Carbohydrates 10.2 g
- Sugar 2.4 g
- Protein 5.1 g
- Cholesterol 3 mg

Crispy Pickles

Preparation Time: 10 minutes
Cooking Time: 6 minutes
Serve: 4

Ingredients:

- 16 dill pickles, sliced
- 1 egg, lightly beaten
- 1/2 cup almond flour
- 3 tbsp parmesan cheese, grated
- 1/2 cup pork rind, crushed

Directions:

1. Take three bowls. Mix together pork rinds and cheese in the first bowl.
2. In a second bowl, add the egg.
3. In the last bowl add the almond flour.
4. Coat each pickle slice with almond flour then dip in egg and finally coat with pork and cheese mixture.
5. Spray air fryer basket with cooking spray.
6. Place coated pickles in the air fryer basket.
7. Cook pickles for 6 minutes at 370 F.
8. Serve and enjoy.

Nutritional Value (Amount per Serving):

- Calories 245
- Fat 17 g
- Carbohydrates 4 g
- Sugar 2 g
- Protein 17 g
- Cholesterol 41 mg

Spiced Green Beans

Preparation Time: 10 minutes
Cooking Time: 10 minutes
Serve: 2

Ingredients:

- 2 cups green beans
- 1/8 tsp cayenne pepper
- 1/8 tsp ground allspice
- 1/4 tsp ground cinnamon
- 1/2 tsp dried oregano
- 2 tbsp olive oil
- 1/4 tsp ground coriander
- 1/4 tsp ground cumin
- 1/2 tsp salt

Directions:

1. Add all ingredients into the large bowl and toss well.
2. Spray air fryer basket with cooking spray.
3. Add bowl mixture into the air fryer basket.
4. Cook at 370 F for 10 minutes. Shake basket halfway through
5. Serve and enjoy.

Nutritional Value (Amount per Serving):

- Calories 155
- Fat 14 g
- Carbohydrates 8 g
- Sugar 1 g
- Protein 2 g
- Cholesterol 0 mg

Creamy Spinach

Preparation Time: 10 minutes
Cooking Time: 16 minutes
Serve: 6

Ingredients:

- 1 lb fresh spinach
- 6 oz gouda cheese, shredded
- 8 oz cream cheese
- 1 tsp garlic powder
- 1 tbsp onion, minced
- Pepper
- Salt

Directions:

1. Preheat the air fryer to 370 F.
2. Spray air fryer baking dish with cooking spray and set aside.
3. Spray a large pan with cooking spray and heat over medium heat.
4. Add spinach to the pan and cook until wilted.
5. Add cream cheese, garlic powder, and onion and stir until cheese is melted.
6. Remove pan from heat and add Gouda cheese and season with pepper and salt.
7. Transfer spinach mixture to the prepared baking dish and place into the air fryer.
8. Cook for 16 minutes.
9. Serve and enjoy.

Nutritional Value (Amount per Serving):

- Calories 255
- Fat 21.3 g
- Carbohydrates 5 g
- Sugar 1.2 g
- Protein 12 g
- Cholesterol 74 mg

Curried Sweet Potato Fries

Preparation Time: 10 minutes
Cooking Time: 20 minutes
Serve: 3

Ingredients:

- 2 sweet potatoes, peeled and cut into fries shape
- 1/4 tsp ground coriander
- 1/2 tsp curry powder
- 2 tbsp olive oil
- Pepper
- Salt

Directions:

1. Add all ingredients into the mixing bowl and toss to coat.
2. Transfer sweet potato fries into the air fryer basket and cook at 370 F for 20 minutes. Toss halfway through.
3. Serve and enjoy.

Nutritional Value (Amount per Serving):

- Calories 118
- Fat 9 g
- Carbohydrates 9 g
- Sugar 2 g
- Protein 1 g
- Cholesterol 0 mg

Spicy Buffalo Cauliflower

Preparation Time: 10 minutes
Cooking Time: 15 minutes
Serve: 4

Ingredients:

- 8 oz cauliflower florets
- 1 tsp cayenne pepper
- 1 tsp chili powder
- 1 tsp olive oil
- 1 tsp garlic, minced
- 1 tomato, diced
- 6 tbsp almond flour
- 1 tsp black pepper
- 1/2 tsp salt

Directions:

1. Preheat the air fryer to 350 F.
2. Spray air fryer basket with cooking spray.
3. Add tomato, garlic, black pepper, olive oil, cayenne pepper, and chili powder into the blender and blend until smooth.
4. Add cauliflower florets into the bowl. Season with pepper and salt.
5. Pour blended mixture over cauliflower florets and toss well to coat.
6. Coat cauliflower florets with almond flour and place into the air fryer basket and cook for 15 minutes. Shake basket 2-3 times.
7. Serve and enjoy.

Nutritional Value (Amount per Serving):

- Calories 92
- Fat 6 g
- Carbohydrates 7 g
- Sugar 2 g
- Protein 3 g
- Cholesterol 0 mg

Ricotta Mushrooms

Preparation Time: 10 minutes
Cooking Time: 12 minutes
Serve: 4

Ingredients:

- 4 large Portobello mushrooms caps
- 1 tbsp olive oil
- 1/4 cup parmesan cheese, grated
- 1/4 tsp rosemary, chopped
- 1 cup spinach, chopped
- 1/4 cup ricotta cheese

Directions:

1. Coat mushrooms with olive oil.
2. Transfer mushrooms into the air fryer basket and cook at 350 F for 2 minutes.
3. In a bowl, mix together remaining ingredients.
4. Stuff bowl mixture into the mushrooms and place into the air fryer basket and cook for 10 minutes more.
5. Serve and enjoy.

Nutritional Value (Amount per Serving):

- Calories 69
- Fat 5.1 g
- Carbohydrates 2.2 g
- Sugar 0.1 g
- Protein 3.5 g
- Cholesterol 6 mg

Parmesan Dill Mushrooms

Preparation Time: 10 minutes

Cooking Time: 8 minutes

Serve: 4

Ingredients:

- 10 mushrooms
- 1 tbsp olive oil
- 2 tbsp mozzarella cheese, grated
- 1 tbsp Italian seasoning
- 2 tbsp cheddar cheese, grated
- 1 tbsp dill, chopped
- Pepper
- Salt

Directions:

1. In a bowl, mix together mushrooms, oil, dill, Italian seasoning, pepper, and salt.
2. Add mushrooms into the air fryer basket and sprinkle cheddar and mozzarella cheese on top.
3. Cook at 350 F for 8 minutes.
4. Serve and enjoy.

Nutritional Value (Amount per Serving):

- Calories 107
- Fat 8.4 g
- Carbohydrates 2.9 g
- Sugar 1.1 g
- Protein 6.5 g
- Cholesterol 14 mg

Roasted Cauliflower & Broccoli

Preparation Time: 10 minutes
Cooking Time: 15 minutes
Serve: 6

Ingredients:

- 3 cups cauliflower florets
- 3 cups broccoli florets
- 1/4 tsp paprika
- 1/2 tsp garlic powder
- 2 tbsp olive oil
- 1/8 tsp pepper
- 1/4 tsp sea salt

Directions:

1. Preheat the air fryer to 400 F.
2. Add broccoli in microwave-safe bowl and microwave for 3 minutes. Drain well.
3. Add broccoli in a large mixing bowl. Add remaining ingredients and toss well.
4. Transfer broccoli and cauliflower mixture into the air fryer basket and cook for 12 minutes.
5. Toss halfway through.
6. Serve and enjoy.

Nutritional Value (Amount per Serving):

- Calories 69
- Fat 4.9 g
- Carbohydrates 5.9 g
- Sugar 2 g
- Protein 2.3 g
- Cholesterol 0 mg

Chapter 8: Desserts Recipes

Cappuccino Muffins

Preparation Time: 10 minutes
Cooking Time: 20 minutes
Serve: 12

Ingredients:

- 4 eggs
- 2 cups almond flour
- 1/2 tsp vanilla
- 1 tsp espresso powder
- 1/2 cup sour cream
- 1 tsp cinnamon
- 2 tsp baking powder
- 1/4 cup coconut flour
- 1/2 cup Swerve
- 1/4 tsp salt

Directions:

1. Preheat the air fryer to 325 F.
2. Add sour cream, vanilla, espresso powder, and eggs in a blender and blend until smooth.
3. Add almond flour, cinnamon, baking powder, coconut flour, sweetener, and salt. Blend again until smooth.
4. Pour batter into the silicone muffin molds and place into the air fryer basket. (Cook in batches)
5. Cook muffins for 20 minutes.
6. Serve and enjoy.

Nutritional Value (Amount per Serving):

- Calories 150
- Fat 13 g
- Carbohydrates 5.3 g
- Sugar 0.8 g
- Protein 6 g
- Cholesterol 59 mg

Tasty Peanut Butter Bars

Preparation Time: 10 minutes
Cooking Time: 24 minutes
Serve: 9

Ingredients:

- 2 eggs
- 1 tbsp coconut flour
- 1/2 cup butter, softened
- 1/2 cup peanut butter
- 1/4 cup almond flour
- 1/2 cup swerve

Directions:

1. Spray air fryer baking pan with cooking spray and set aside.
2. In a bowl, beat together butter, eggs, and peanut butter until well combined.
3. Add dry ingredients and mix until a smooth batter is formed.
4. Spread batter evenly in prepared pan and place into the air fryer and cook at 325 F for 24 minutes.
5. Slice and serve.

Nutritional Value (Amount per Serving):

- Calories 215
- Fat 20 g
- Carbohydrates 4 g
- Sugar 2 g
- Protein 6 g
- Cholesterol 26 mg

Choco Mug Cake

Preparation Time: 5 minutes
Cooking Time: 20 minutes
Serve: 1

Ingredients:

- 1 egg, lightly beaten
- 1 tbsp heavy cream
- ¼ tsp baking powder
- 2 tbsp unsweetened cocoa powder
- 2 tbsp Erythritol
- ½ tsp vanilla
- 1 tbsp peanut butter
- 1 tsp salt

Directions:

1. Preheat the air fryer to 400 F.
2. In a bowl, mix together all ingredients until well combined.
3. Spray mug with cooking spray.
4. Pour batter in mug and place in the air fryer and cook for 20 minutes.
5. Serve and enjoy.

Nutritional Value (Amount per Serving):

- Calories 241
- Fat 19 g
- Carbohydrates 10 g
- Sugar 2 g
- Protein 12 g
- Cholesterol 184 mg

Coconut Berry Pudding

Preparation Time: 10 minutes
Cooking Time: 15 minutes
Serve: 6

Ingredients:

- 2 cups coconut cream
- 1 lime zest, grated
- 3 tbsp erythritol
- ¼ cup blueberries
- 1/3 cup blackberries

Directions:

1. Add all ingredients into the blender and blend until well combined.
2. Spray 6 ramekins with cooking spray.
3. Pour blended mixture into the ramekins and place in the air fryer.
4. Cook at 340 F for 15 minutes.
5. Serve and enjoy.

Nutritional Value (Amount per Serving):

- Calories 190
- Fat 19 g
- Carbohydrates 6 g
- Sugar 3.7 g
- Protein 2 g
- Cholesterol 0 mg

Coconut Pie

Preparation Time: 10 minutes
Cooking Time: 12 minutes
Serve: 6

Ingredients:

- 2 eggs
- 1/2 cup coconut flour
- 1/2 cup erythritol
- 1 cup shredded coconut
- 1 1/2 tsp vanilla
- 1/4 cup butter
- 1 1/2 cups coconut milk

Directions:

1. Add all ingredients into the large bowl and mix until well combined.
2. Spray a 6-inch baking dish with cooking spray.
3. Pour batter into the prepared dish and place in the air fryer basket.
4. Cook at 350 F for 10-12 minutes.
5. Slice and serve.

Nutritional Value (Amount per Serving):

- Calories 282
- Fat 28.9 g
- Carbohydrates 6.3 g
- Sugar 3.2 g
- Protein 4 g
- Cholesterol 75 mg

Strawberry Cheese Cake

Preparation Time: 10 minutes
Cooking Time: 35 minutes
Serve: 6

Ingredients:

- 1 cup almond flour
- 3 tbsp coconut oil, melted
- ½ tsp vanilla
- 1 egg, lightly beaten
- 1 tbsp fresh lime juice
- ¼ cup erythritol
- 1 cup cream cheese, softened
- 1 lb strawberries, chopped
- 2 tsp baking powder

Directions:

1. Add all ingredients into the large bowl and mix until well combined.
2. Spray air fryer cake pan with cooking spray.
3. Pour batter into the prepared pan and place into the air fryer and cook at 350 F for 35 minutes.
4. Allow to cool completely.
5. Slice and serve.

Nutritional Value (Amount per Serving):

- Calories 195
- Fat 17.3 g
- Carbohydrates 3.2 g
- Sugar 1 g
- Protein 7.2 g
- Cholesterol 52 mg

Ricotta Cheese Cake

Preparation Time: 10 minutes
Cooking Time: 30 minutes
Serve: 8

Ingredients:

- 3 eggs, lightly beaten
- 1 tsp baking powder
- ½ cup ghee, melted
- 1 cup almond flour
- 1/3 cup erythritol
- 1 cup ricotta cheese, soft

Directions:

1. Add all ingredients into the bowl and mix until well combined.
2. Pour batter into the greased air fryer baking dish and place into the air fryer.
3. Cook at 350 F for 30 minutes.
4. Slice and serve.

Nutritional Value (Amount per Serving):

- Calories 259
- Fat 23 g
- Carbohydrates 5 g
- Sugar 0.5 g
- Protein 8 g
- Cholesterol 104 mg

Easy Lava Cake

Preparation Time: 10 minutes

Cooking Time: 9 minutes

Serve: 2

Ingredients:

- 1 egg
- 1/2 tsp baking powder
- 1 tbsp coconut oil, melted
- 1 tbsp flax meal
- 2 tbsp erythritol
- 2 tbsp water
- 2 tbsp unsweetened cocoa powder
- Pinch of salt

Directions:

1. Whisk all ingredients into the bowl and transfer in two ramekins.
2. Preheat the air fryer to 350 F.
3. Place ramekins in air fryer basket and bake for 8-9 minutes.
4. Carefully remove ramekins from air fryer and let it cool for 10 minutes.
5. Serve and enjoy.

Nutritional Value (Amount per Serving):

- Calories 119
- Fat 11 g
- Carbohydrates 4 g
- Sugar 0.3 g
- Protein 5 g
- Cholesterol 82 mg

Pumpkin Cookies

Preparation Time: 10 minutes
Cooking Time: 20 minutes
Serve: 27

Ingredients:

- 1 egg
- 2 cups almond flour
- 1/2 tsp baking powder
- 1 tsp vanilla
- 1/2 cup butter
- 15 drops liquid stevia
- 1/2 tsp pumpkin pie spice
- 1/2 cup pumpkin puree

Directions:

1. Preheat the air fryer to 280 F.
2. In a large bowl, add all ingredients and mix until well combined.
3. Make cookies from mixture and place into the air fryer and cook for 20 minutes.
4. Serve and enjoy.

Nutritional Value (Amount per Serving):

- Calories 80
- Fat 7 g
- Carbohydrates 2 g
- Sugar 1 g
- Protein 3 g
- Cholesterol 25 mg

Almond Pumpkin Cookies

Preparation Time: 10 minutes
Cooking Time: 8 minutes
Serve: 8

Ingredients:

- ¼ cup almond flour
- ½ cup pumpkin puree
- 3 tbsp swerve
- ½ tsp baking soda
- 1 tbsp coconut flakes
- ½ tsp cinnamon
- Pinch of salt

Directions:

1. Preheat the air fryer to 360 F.
2. Add all ingredients into the bowl and mix until well combined.
3. Spray air fryer basket with cooking spray.
4. Make cookies from bowl mixture and place into the air fryer and cook for 8 minutes.
5. Serve and enjoy.

Nutritional Value (Amount per Serving):

- Calories 30
- Fat 2 g
- Carbohydrates 3 g
- Sugar 0.7 g
- Protein 1 g
- Cholesterol 0 mg

Almond Cinnamon Mug Cake

Preparation Time: 5 minutes
Cooking Time: 10 minutes
Serve: 1

Ingredients:

- 1 scoop vanilla protein powder
- 1/2 tsp cinnamon
- 1 tsp granulated sweetener
- 1 tbsp almond flour
- 1/2 tsp baking powder
- 1/4 tsp vanilla
- 1/4 cup unsweetened almond milk

Directions:

1. Add protein powder, cinnamon, almond flour, sweetener, and baking powder into the mug and mix well.
2. Add vanilla and almond milk and stir well.
3. Place mug in the air fryer and cook at 390 F for 10 minutes
4. Serve and enjoy.

Nutritional Value (Amount per Serving):

- Calories 181
- Fat 6 g
- Carbohydrates 8 g
- Sugar 2 g
- Protein 23 g
- Cholesterol 31 mg

Crustless Pie

Preparation Time: 10 minutes
Cooking Time: 24 minutes
Serve: 4

Ingredients:

- 3 eggs
- 1/2 cup pumpkin puree
- 1/2 tsp cinnamon
- 1 tsp vanilla
- 1/4 cup erythritol
- 1/2 cup cream
- 1/2 cup unsweetened almond milk

Directions:

1. Preheat the air fryer to 325 F.
2. Spray air fryer baking dish with cooking spray and set aside.
3. In a large bowl, add all ingredients and beat until smooth.
4. Pour pie mixture into the prepared dish and place into the air fryer and cook for 24 minutes.
5. Let it cool completely and place into the refrigerator for 1-2 hours.
6. Slice and serve.

Nutritional Value (Amount per Serving):

- Calories 85
- Fat 5 g
- Carbohydrates 4 g
- Sugar 1 g
- Protein 5 g
- Cholesterol 35 mg

Pumpkin Custard

Preparation Time: 10 minutes
Cooking Time: 32 minutes
Serve: 6

Ingredients:

- 4 egg yolks
- 1/2 tsp cinnamon
- 15 drops liquid stevia
- 15 oz pumpkin puree
- 3/4 cup coconut cream
- 1/8 tsp cloves
- 1/8 tsp ginger

Directions:

1. Preheat the air fryer to 325 F.
2. In a large bowl, combine together pumpkin puree, cinnamon, swerve, cloves, and ginger.
3. Add egg yolks and beat until combined.
4. Add coconut cream and stir well.
5. Pour mixture into the six ramekins and place into the air fryer.
6. Cook for 32 minutes.
7. Let it cool completely then place in the refrigerator.
8. Serve chilled and enjoy.

Nutritional Value (Amount per Serving):

- Calories 131
- Fat 11 g
- Carbohydrates 3 g
- Sugar 2 g
- Protein 4 g
- Cholesterol 12 mg

Conclusion

Make the most of the air fryer is changing the way today's family cooking. This all-new Indian cookbook features variety of quick dinners and simple snacks. Looking for crispy fried chicken without all the fat? You also get side dishes that free up the range, kid-pleasing bites, and fresh air fried treats for lazy mornings. Air fry all of these family favorites and more without the mess, time, fat or worry.

If you have an air fryer at home, then you will also get to find all the Indian recipes that you can cook in your air fryer in no time!

CPSIA information can be obtained
at www.ICGtesting.com
Printed in the USA
LVHW062022231221
706911LV00005B/157

9 781915 038494